HYMNUS PARADISI

HERBERT HOWELLS

Hymnus Paradisi

for soprano & tenor soli, SATB & orchestra

NOVELLO PUBLISHING LIMITED

HYMNUS PARADISI

I
PRELUDIO

II
REQUIEM AETERNAM

REQUIEM aeternam dona eis,
Et lux perpetua luceat eis.

III
THE LORD IS MY SHEPHERD

THE Lord is my shepherd : therefore can I lack nothing.

He shall feed me in a green pasture : and lead me forth beside the waters of comfort.

He shall convert my soul : and bring me forth in the paths of righteousness.

Yea, though I walk through the valley of the shadow of death, I will fear no evil : thy rod and thy staff comfort me.

Thou shalt prepare a table before me against them that trouble me : thou hast anointed my head with oil, and my cup shall be full.

But thy loving kindness and mercy shall follow me all the days of my life : and I will dwell in the house of the Lord for ever.

Psalm 23.

IV
SANCTUS
I WILL LIFT UP MINE EYES

SANCTUS, Sanctus, Sanctus, Dominus Deus Sabaoth.
Pleni sunt coeli et terra gloria tua.

I WILL lift up mine eyes unto the hills : from whence cometh my help.

My help cometh even from the Lord : who hath made heaven and earth.

He will not suffer thy foot to be moved : and he that keepeth thee will not sleep.

Behold, he that keepeth Israel : shall neither slumber nor sleep.

The Lord himself is thy keeper : the Lord is thy defence upon thy right hand ;

So that the sun shall not burn thee by day : neither the moon by night.

The Lord shall preserve thee from all evil : yea, it is even he that shall keep thy soul.

The Lord shall preserve thy going out, and thy coming in : from this time forth for evermore.

Psalm 121.

V

I HEARD A VOICE FROM HEAVEN

I HEARD a voice from heaven, saying unto me, Write, From henceforth blessed are the dead which die in the Lord : even so saith the Spirit ; for they rest from their labours.

From the Burial Service.

VI

HOLY IS THE TRUE LIGHT

HOLY is the true light, and passing wonderful, lending radiance to them that endured in the heat of the conflict : from Christ they inherit a home of unfading splendour, wherein they rejoice with gladness evermore. Alleluia.

From the Salisbury Diurnal,
Translated by Dr. G. H. Palmer.

REQUIEM aeternam,
Requiem dona eis sempiternam.

INSTRUMENTATION

2 Flutes (2nd plays Piccolo*)
2 Oboes
Cor Anglais*
2 Clarinets
Bass Clarinet*
2 Bassoons
Double Bassoon*

4 Horns
3 Trumpets
2 Tenor Trombones
Bass Trombone
Tuba

Timpani

Bass Drum and Cymbals

Harp
Piano*
Celesta*
Organ*

Strings

Instruments marked * can be omitted
Time of performance approximately 48 minutes

HYMNUS PARADISI

for Soprano and Tenor Soli, Chorus and Orchestra

HERBERT HOWELLS

I
PRELUDIO

17468
Copyright, 1950, by Novello & Company, Limited

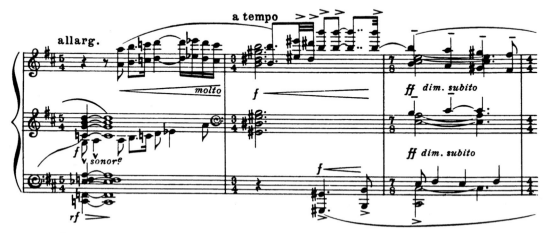

II
REQUIEM AETERNAM

*Passages within brackets are for voices alone.

4

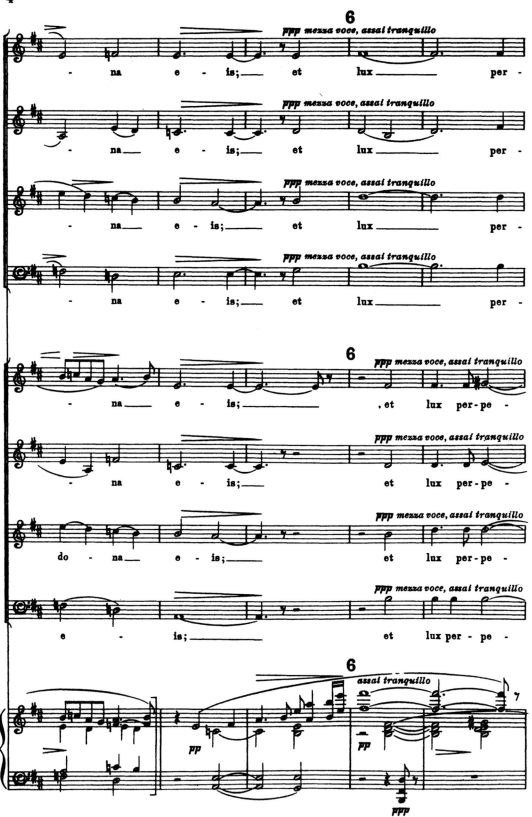

6

lux per-pe - - - tua lu - ce - at

lux per-pe - - tu-a lu - ce - at

lux per-pe - - tu-a lu - ce - at

lux per-pe - - tu-a lu - ce - at

is, et lux per-pe - tua lu - ce - at

is, et lux per-pe-tu-a lu - ce - at

is, et lux per-pe-tu-a lu - ce - at

is, et lux per-pe-tu-a lu - ce - at

9

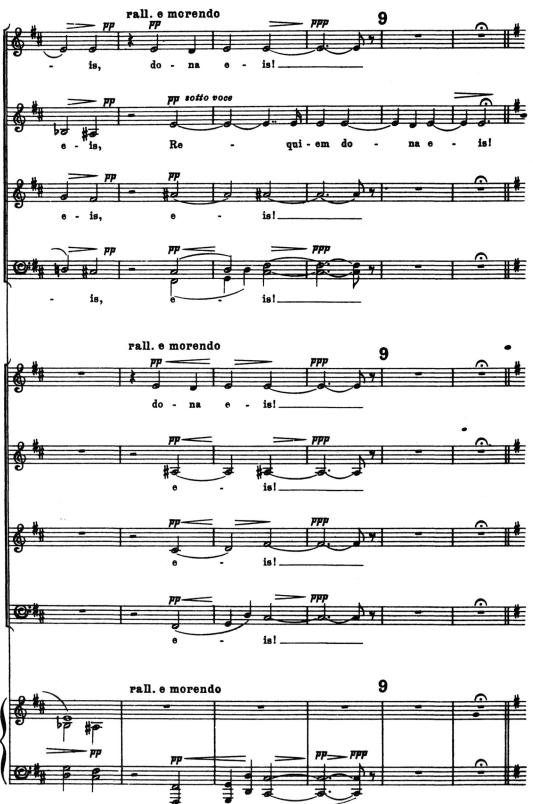

SOPRANO SOLO placido, teneramente (ma più mosso) ♩ = 86

p dolce

Re - qui - em_____ ae - ter - nam

do - na_____ e - is, et lux_ per - pe -

10

- tua lu - ce-at e - - -

- - is! _____

16

17468

19

17468

22

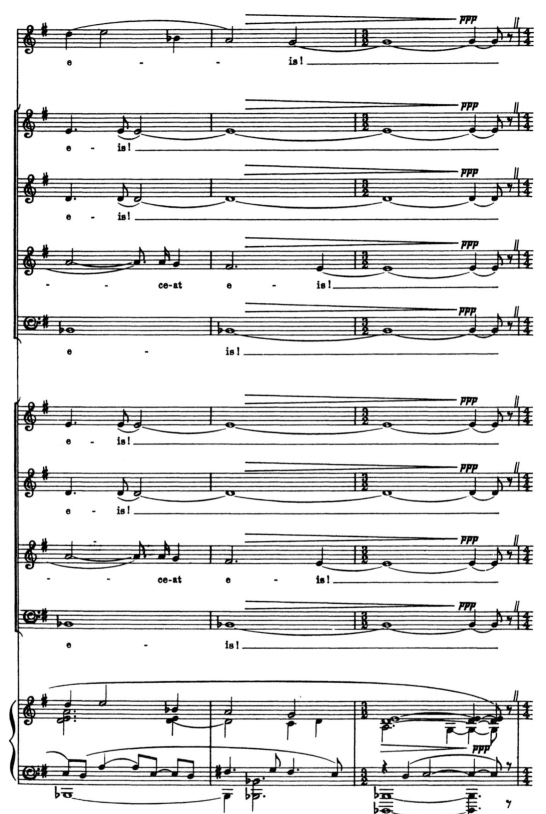

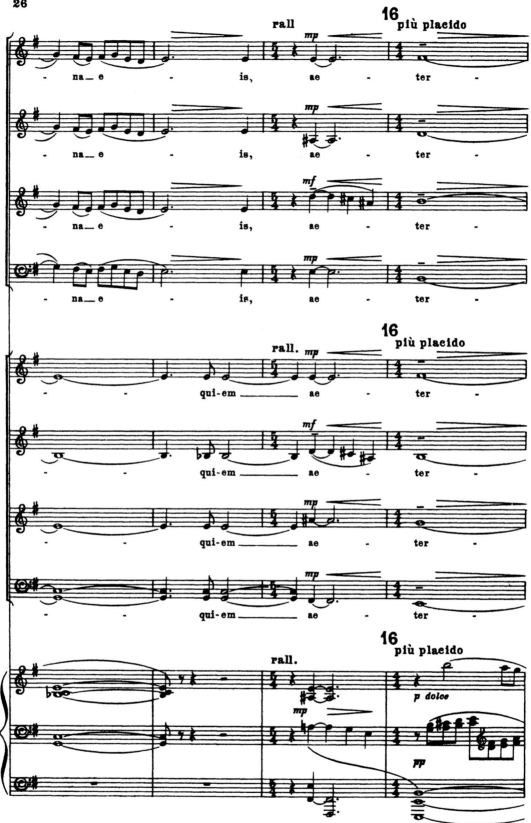

III
THE LORD IS MY SHEPHERD

shall con - vert ___ my ___ soul: ___ and lead me forth ___

paths of right - eousness.

20 poco allarg. a tempo

be - side ___ the wa - ters of com -

The Lord ___ is ___ my ___ shep - herd:

20 poco allarg. a tempo

The Lord is my ___ shep - herd: there - fore ___

The Lord is my shep - herd: there - fore ___

The Lord is my shep - herd: there - fore ___

There - fore

There - fore

poco allarg. a tempo

20

34

22

38

shall fol-low me___ all the days of my life:___ and I will dwell___ in the

in tempo ♩ = c. 52

house_____ of the Lord____ for ev - er, for ev -

26

- er.___

26

mp
But thy lov-ing-kind-ness and

mp
But thy lov-ing-kind-ness and

mp
But thy lov-ing-kind-ness and

mp
But thy lov-ing-kind-ness and

26

17468

40

17468

IV
SANCTUS
I WILL LIFT UP MINE EYES

SOPRANO SOLO ♩= 92

mf dolce, flebile

I will lift up mine eyes unto the

- ctus,

- ctus,

- ctus,

p dolce, flebile

col Ped.

hills: from whence com-eth my help.

San - ctus.

San -

ALTO I

San -

mf *dim.*

46

17468

54

He will not suf-fer thy foot_ to be moved:_____ and he that
He will not suf-fer thy foot_ to be moved:_____ and he that
He will not suf-fer thy foot_ to be moved:_____ and he that
He will not suf-fer thy foot_ to be moved:_____ and he that

39

keep-eth thee will not sleep._____ Be-hold,_____ he that keep-eth
keep-eth thee will not sleep._____ Be-hold, he that keep - eth
keep-eth thee will not sleep._____ Be-hold, he that keep - eth
keep-eth thee_ will not sleep._____ Be-hold, he that keep - eth

39

58

17468

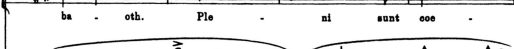

61

17468

62

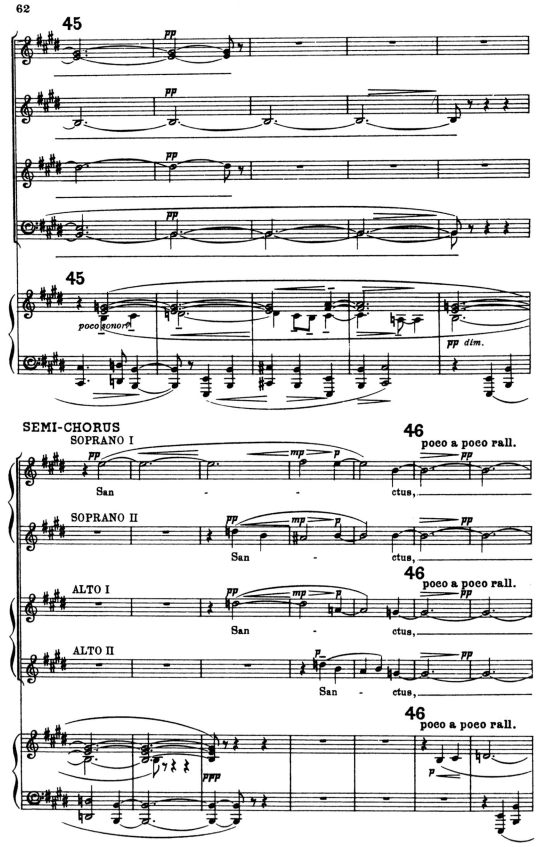

SEMI-CHORUS

SOPRANO I

SOPRANO II

ALTO I

ALTO II

17468

65

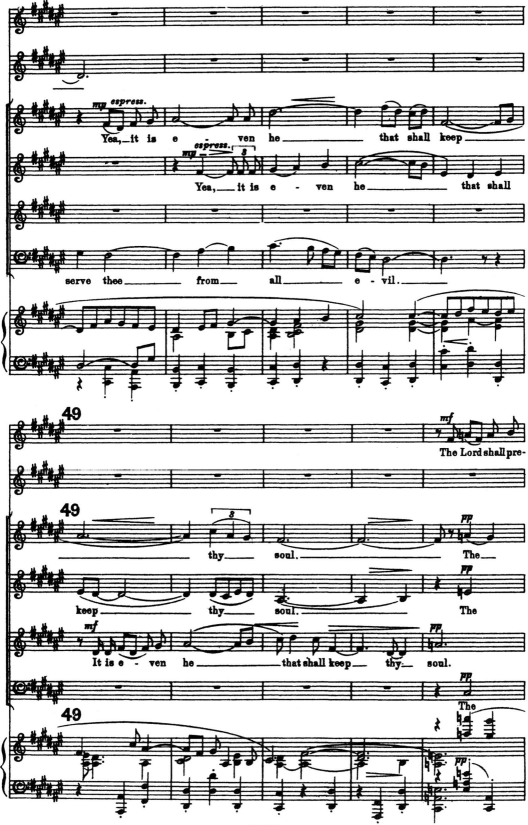

66

17468

68

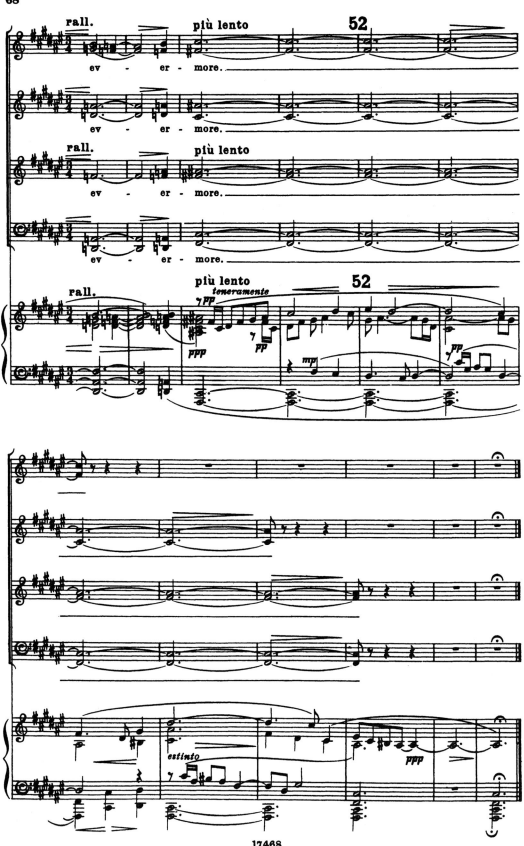

V
I HEARD A VOICE FROM HEAVEN

70

17468

73

17468

74

17468

VI
HOLY IS THE TRUE LIGHT

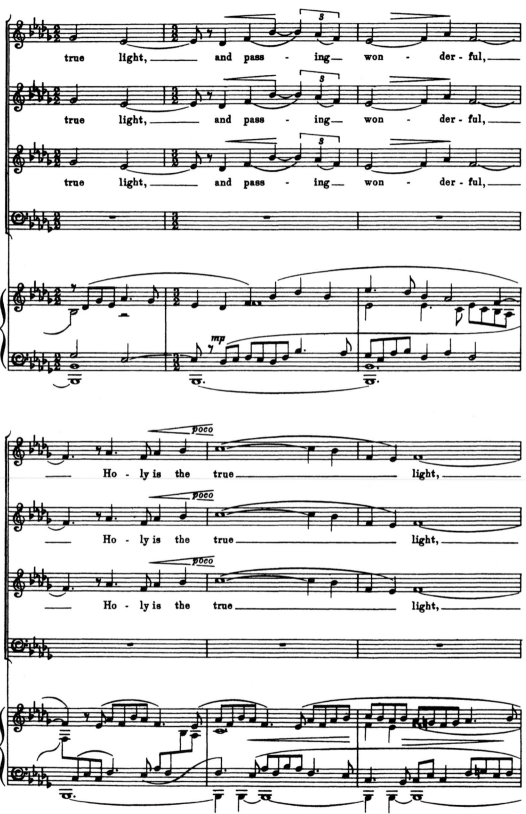

80

sempre più con moto ed accel.

Al - le - lu -

lu - ia,

sempre più con moto ed accel.

- le - lu - ia, Al -

Al - le - lu -

sempre più con moto ed accel.

ia, _____

Al - le - lu - ia, Al - le -

- le - lu - ia, _____

ia, Al - le - lu -

sonoro

and pass-ing won - der-ful, _____ lend - ing

and won - der-ful, _____

and won - der-ful, _____

and won - der-ful, _____

66

ra - diance ___ to them that en - dured ___ in the heat of the

lend - ing ra - diance to them that en - dured the

lend - ing ___ ra - diance _____ to them that en-

88

17468

89

17468

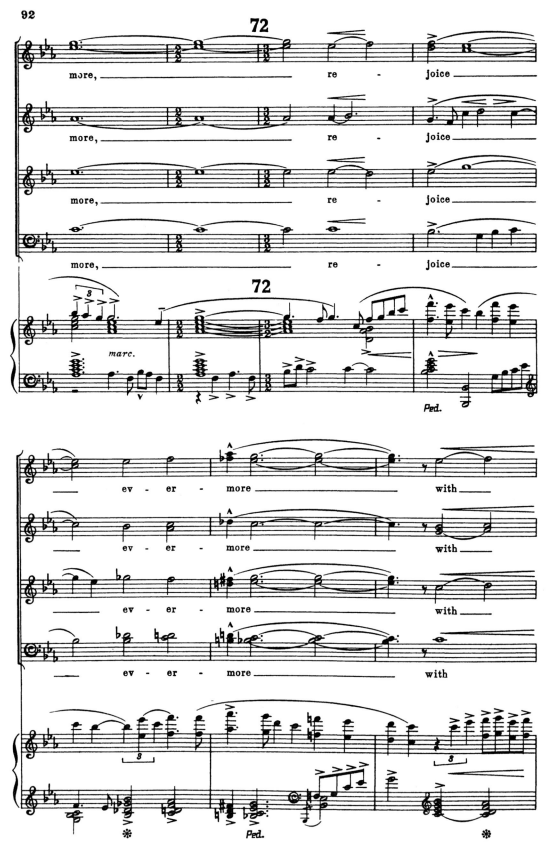

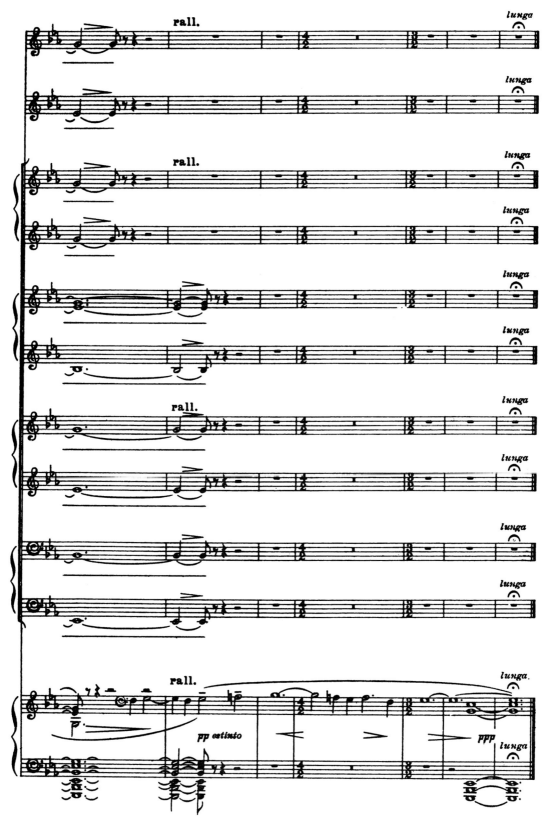

Published by Novello & Company Limited
Printed in Great Britain

HERBERT HOWELLS

ANTHEMS AND MOTETS

BEHOLD, O GOD, OUR DEFENDER
SATB and organ
A HYMN FOR ST CECILIA
SATB and organ
KING OF GLORY
SATB and organ
I LOVE ALL BEAUTEOUS THINGS
SATB and organ
ONE THING HAVE I DESIRED
SATB with divisions
REGINA CAELI
SSAATTBB
REQUIEM
STBar soli, SSAATTBB
SALVE REGINA and O SALUTARIS HOSTIA
SSATBB and SATB
THEE WILL I LOVE
SATB and organ
WHERE WAST THOU?
Bar solo, SATB and organ

EVENING SERVICES

CHICHESTER CATHEDRAL
SATB and organ
COLLEGIUM REGALE
SATB and organ
GLOUCESTER CATHEDRAL
SATB and organ
ST AUGUSTINIES'S, BIRMINGHAM
SATB and organ
ST JOHN'S COLLEGE, CAMBRIDGE
SATB and organ
ST PAUL'S CATHEDRAL
SATB and organ
ST PETER, WESTMINSTER
SATB and organ
WESTMINSTER CATHEDRAL - NUNC DIMITTIS ONLY
SSAATTBB unaccompanied
WINCHESTER CATHEDRAL
SATB and organ
WORCESTER CATHEDRAL
SATB and organ
YORK MINSTER
SATB and organ

Novello

918 (90)